# BIG BIBLE BANNERS
# AND ROOM DECORATIONS

## by
## Sally A. Boscaljon

### illustrated by
### Veronica Terrill

Cover by Corbin Hillam

Shining Star Publications, Copyright © 1992
A Division of Good Apple

ISBN No. 0-86653-635-3

Standardized Subject Code TA ac

Printing No. 987654321

**Shining Star Publications**
**A Division of Good Apple**
**1204 Buchanan St., Box 299**
**Carthage, IL 62321-0299**

Unless otherwise indicated, the New International Version of the Bible was used in preparing the activities in this book.

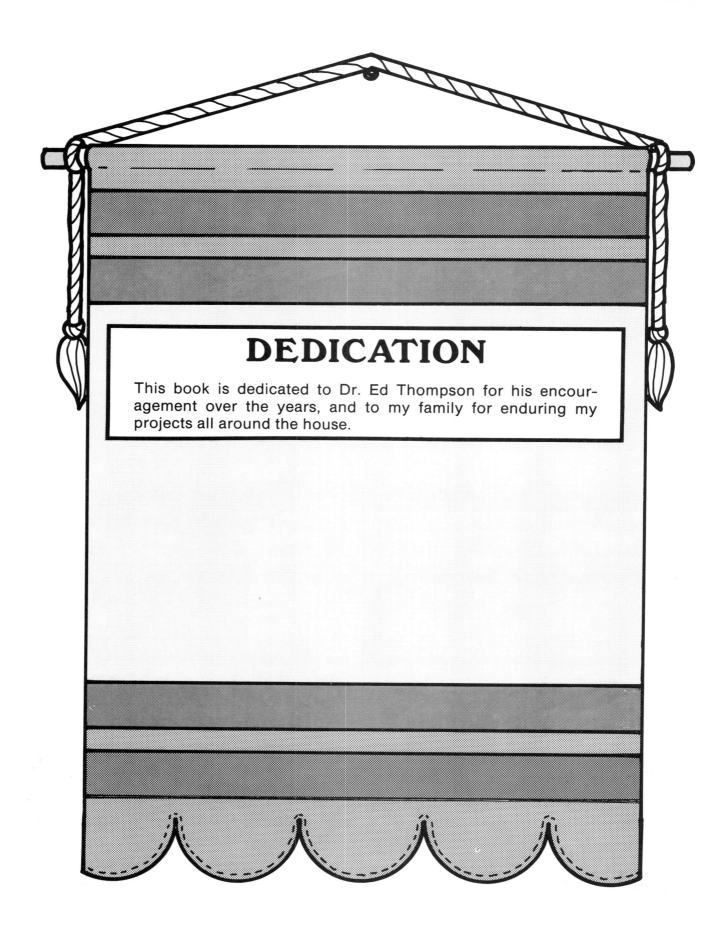

# DEDICATION

This book is dedicated to Dr. Ed Thompson for his encouragement over the years, and to my family for enduring my projects all around the house.

# TABLE OF CONTENTS

Shining Star Publications, Copyright © 1992, A Division of Good Apple                    SS2808

# TIPS FOR THE TEACHER

I have always noticed the designs of churches—the colors, the wood, the windows, the lights, the architectural style and the symbolism. Maybe you have, too, and that's why you're looking at this book!

Before any music begins or a pastor approaches the altar, most worshipers are in the pews, absorbing their surroundings. Appropriate banners can heighten the worship experience by focusing on the theme of the day or helping us focus on the Lord—who He is and what He has done. Let's pray that these banners will make worship more meaningful for many at your church.

The banners in this book can be adjusted to fit the size of your sanctuary. Use an opaque projector or copier to enlarge the designs to suit your situation and modify measurements accordingly. Use your own creativity to adjust the design or Scripture verse to satisfy your taste and suit your situation.

Most of the banners can be used anytime throughout the year. The table of contents gives some suggestions for seasonal use.

Burlap is the basic fabric I chose because the thick threads make it easier to check for straight lines, and a thread can be pulled to mark a hem or cutting line. It is sturdy, adds a nice texture and doesn't get spotty if glue soaks through. My other fabric choice is medium- to heavyweight felt because it doesn't ravel and is easily cut. Other fabric can be used, but be aware of fraying and problems with glue spots.

God created color and shape texture and all the elements of art. It will be a blessing to you to use His elements and your gifts at your church!

BASIC SUPPLIES:

Scissors
Pins
Measuring tape, yardstick, ruler
Opaque projector or copy machine
Glue
Dowels or curtain rods

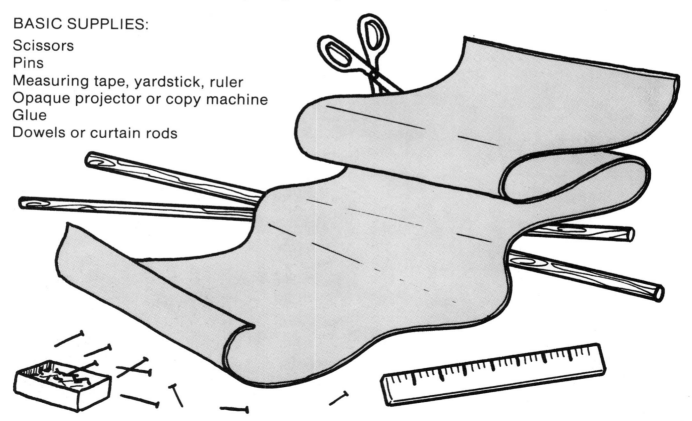

## HELPFUL HINTS:

- Burlap background piece can be cut to size by measuring carefully and pulling a thread to give you a clear cutting line.
- Try laying the background fabric on a clean tile floor and use the squares as a cutting guide for straight lines and square corners.
- A felt background will hold its shape better if you turn back two or three inches for a side hem before putting in a top or bottom hem. Add this hem allowance when purchasing felt to be sure you buy enough fabric. Turn, pin and glue along edge on wrong side.
- Cut letters and shapes and lay out entire banner before gluing any fabric onto background. Adjustments to please your eye and the size of your banner can then be made.
- Run glue very close to the edges of letters or any other design. For larger pieces, use a crisscross pattern of glue and spread with your finger. A bonding material found at fabric stores can be used instead of glue.
- Burlap banners can be lined with a lightweight fabric for added durability. Make the lining piece the same size as the finished banner, then turn under 1-1½" all around, pin and stitch or glue.
- A rod pocket is worked into each design in this book for the top of each banner. A bottom rod will help weigh down the banner and will help pull out any wrinkles missed while pressing and will help it hang straight. Some patterns allow for a bottom rod pocket also.
- Rod choices include stained or painted wooden dowels, cafe rods, or PVC (plumbing pipe). If you choose a cafe rod, measure it to the correct length, drill a hole in the middle and secure with a screw. Holes for a wire hanger should be drilled about 1" from the ends. I suggest cafe rods, usually 1" diameter, because they are nice looking and lightweight; but, they are also the most expensive choice.
- Allow glue to dry thoroughly before moving or hanging your banner.
- Sign your name and date on the back of your banner.
- Banners can be dry-cleaned, but be sure to explain what kind of glue and fabric you used and be prepared for some fix-up work.

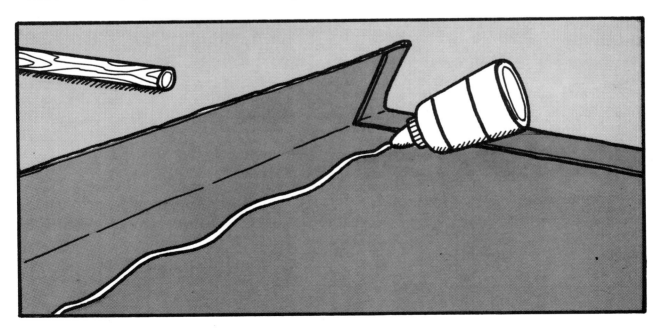

Shining Star Publications, Copyright © 1992, A Division of Good Apple                    SS2808

# LOVE ONE ANOTHER, AS I HAVE LOVED YOU

## JOHN 15:12 KJV

Suggested size 3' x 6' each

## MATERIALS:

Basic supplies (see introduction)
2 3' x 7' pieces burgundy burlap
¾ yard each—felt or other fabric in 3 dark-red or burgundy shades
½ yard white or cream felt
10 yards yarn to match white or cream felt

## INSTRUCTIONS:

- Prepare background burgundy by running a zigzag of glue on wrong side along sides.
- Pull a thread out 6" from the bottom. Remove all threads down to bottom to make fringe. Run a zigzag of glue above fringe to prevent further fraying.
  (NOTE: If using felt or other fabric instead of burlap, purchased fringe or trim may be used at bottom.)
- Pull a thread out 6" from top edge to form hemline. Turn hem to wrong side and glue close to edge. This forms the rod pocket.
- Enlarge patterns using opaque projector or copier.
- Cut two hearts of each shade of red felt.
- Place hearts in columns as shown. Glue in place.
- Cut letters from cream or white felt, arrange on hearts and glue in place.
- Run thread of glue down each side 2" from edge and press yarn onto glue. Allow yarn to hang down at bottom as long as the fringe.
- Run thread of glue in an arch along the top as shown and press yarn onto glue.
- Slide rod into rod pocket and hang.

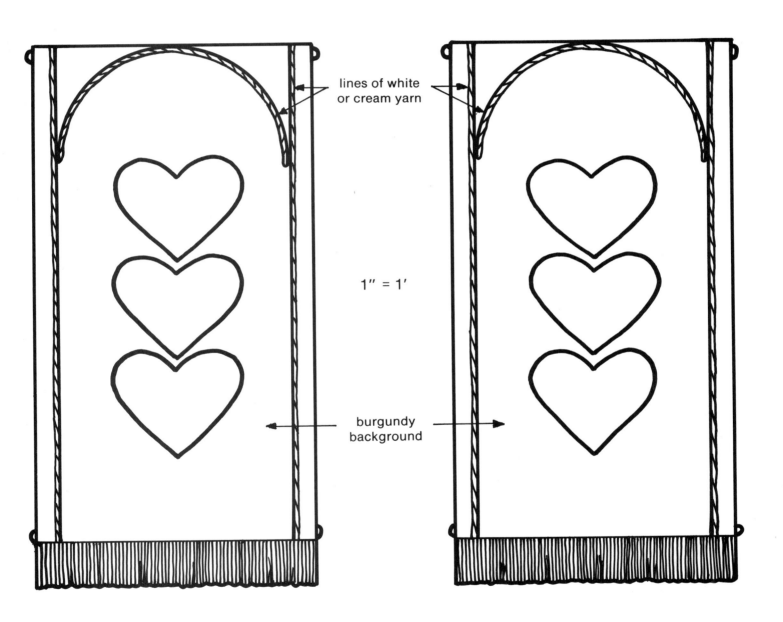

lines of white
or cream yarn

1″ = 1′

burgundy
background

SS2808

# LOVE ONE ANOTHER, AS I HAVE LOVED YOU

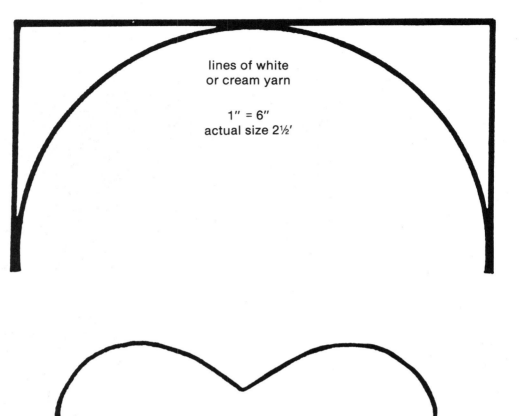

lines of white
or cream yarn

1″ = 6″
actual size 2½′

1″ = 4″
or
actual size 16″ wide

cut six hearts
two of each shade
of dark-red
and burgundy

SS2808

## LOVE ONE ANOTHER, AS I HAVE LOVED YOU

LOVE
ONE
ANOTHER

AS I
HAVE
LOVED
YOU

½″ = 4″
actual size 4″

cream or white
felt letters

½″ = 4″
actual size 4″

# GREATER LOVE HAS NO ONE THAN THIS, THAT HE LAY DOWN HIS LIFE FOR HIS FRIENDS

## JOHN 15:13

Suggested size 3' x 9'

### MATERIALS:

Basic supplies (see introduction)
3½' x 10' lavender felt
3' x 4½' red burlap
3' x 7' black burlap or felt
1 yard green felt
4 yards red rug yarn

### INSTRUCTIONS:

- Prepare lavender background by turning 3" on long sides to back; glue along edges. Measure 6" on top and bottom; turn to back for rod pockets. Glue close to edge.
- Enlarge patterns using an opaque projector or copier.
- Cut heart from red burlap.
- Cut cross and nails from black felt.
- Cut letters from green felt.
- Place heart in position on lavender background. Glue in place. Fold at dotted lines and glue to wrong side.
- Place cross on top of heart as shown. Glue in place. Fold at dotted line and turn to back side; glue.
- Glue nails in place.
- Position letters, noting that each *A* is lowered about 1" and each *O* is raised from line of lettering. Glue in place.
- Run thread of glue 2" above top edge of heart and press red yarn onto glue.
- Run thread of glue along bottom edge of heart, extending down around lower leg of cross and press red yarn in place.
- Slide rods into rod pockets and hang.

GREATER LOVE HAS NO ONE THAN THIS, THAT HE LAY DOWN HIS LIFE FOR HIS FRIENDS

10

SS2808

1″ = 1′

SS2808

# GREATER LOVE HAS NO ONE THAN THIS,
## THAT HE LAY DOWN HIS LIFE FOR HIS FRIENDS

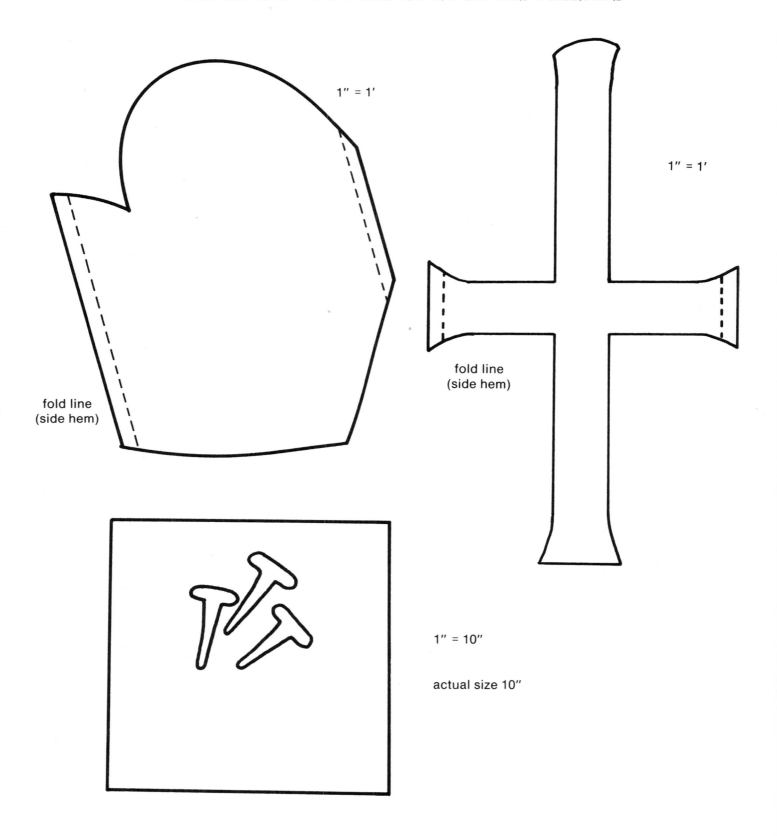

1″ = 1′

1″ = 1′

fold line
(side hem)

fold line
(side hem)

1″ = 10″

actual size 10″

**GREATER LOVE HAS NO ONE THAN THIS, THAT HE LAY DOWN HIS LIFE FOR HIS FRIENDS**

¾″ = 8″
or
actual size 8″

GREATER
LOVE
HAS
NO ONE
THAN THIS,
THAT HE LAY DOWN
HIS LIFE FOR
HIS FRIENDS

# ALLELUIA!

## BASED ON REVELATION 19:1

Suggested size 3' x 9'

MATERIALS:

Basic supplies (see introduction)
3½' x 8¾' bright-orange felt
2' x 8½' yellow felt
12" x 24" red felt
12" x 36" orange felt (different color from background)
12" x 24" yellow felt or scraps from cross
12" x 24" taupe, or yellow-green felt
12" x 24" black felt
1 skein black rug yarn

INSTRUCTIONS:

- Turn back the side hems of orange background 3"; glue close to edge.
- Turn back upper hem 6" for rod pocket; glue close to edge.
- Enlarge patterns using opaque projector or copier.
- Cut shapes from colored felt as indicated on page 16.
- Cut out long yellow strip (shape #13) and letters.
- Glue on long yellow strip.
- Arrange other shapes around as shown in picture and glue.
- Arrange letters as shown and glue.
- Run a thread of glue around edges of all the shapes (except long yellow vertical strip) and press black yarn in place.
- Cut 14 pieces of rug yarn 1½' long.
- Make pompons by wrapping yarn loosely around first four fingers 30 times. Slip off fingers and tie in the middle. Cut through loops. Separate the strands to make a fluffy pompon.
- Securely tie pompons to the lengths of rug yarn.
- Working on wrong side of banner, turn 3" bottom hem toward wrong side.
- Slip the 14 lengths of yarn into the hem with the pompons toward the top of banner and glue hem catching the yarn.
- Allow glue to dry.
- Fold yarn lengths toward bottom edge of banner with the pompons dangling below. Glue yarn in place at bottom edge of banner.
- Slip rod into rod pocket and hang.

# ALLELUIA!

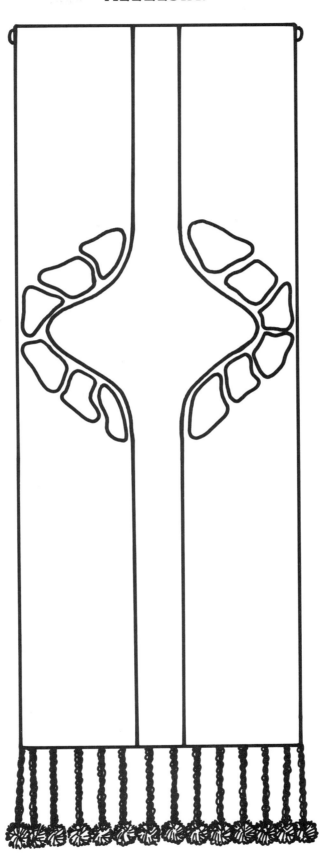

1″ = 1′

SS2808

# ALLELUIA!

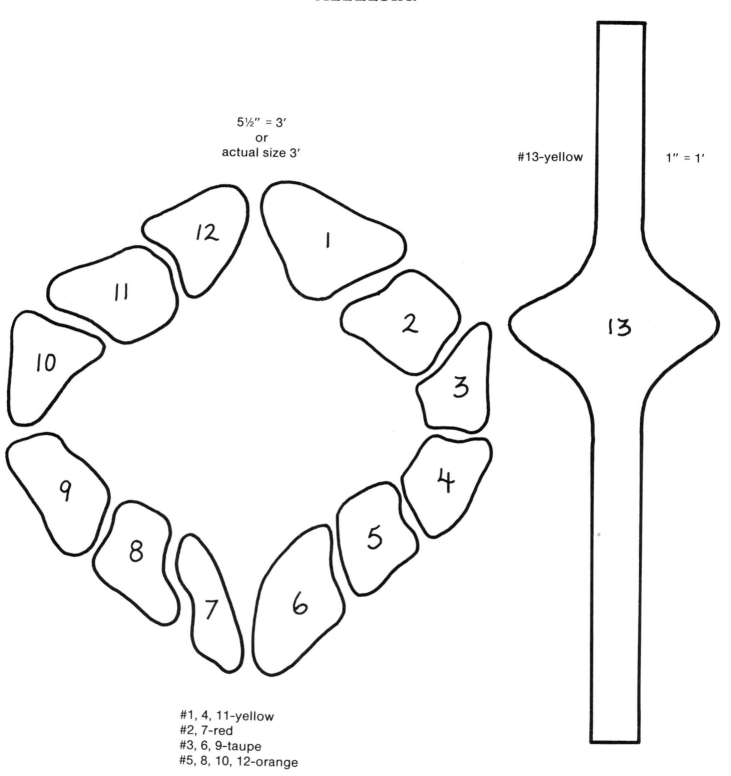

5½″ = 3′
or
actual size 3′

#13-yellow

1″ = 1′

#1, 4, 11-yellow
#2, 7-red
#3, 6, 9-taupe
#5, 8, 10, 12-orange

16

SS2808

# ALLELUIA!

actual size
small letters-4″
large letters-6″

letters black

SS2808

# HE IS RISEN!

## BASED ON LUKE 24:6

Suggested size 3' x 10'

MATERIALS:

Basic supplies (see introduction)
3' x 11' orange burlap
2 yards 45"-wide yellow felt
1 yard dark-orange felt
½ yard white felt
1 yard black felt
10 yards black yarn
Gold, yellow and orange felt scraps

INSTRUCTIONS:

- Prepare orange background by running a zigzag of glue around edges to prevent fraying.
- Pull thread 6" from top and bottom to form hemlines. Fold to back and glue close to edge.
- Enlarge patterns using opaque projector or copier.
- Cut butterfly wings #4, background for words section #6 and shape for very bottom #7 from yellow felt.
- Cut very top shape #8, one of #1 and one of #9, from dark-orange felt.
- Cut one #1 from white felt.
- Cut wing edges #5 and body #2 from black felt.
- Cut letters from black felt.
- Cut little spots #3 from yellow, orange and gold scraps.
- Position pieces as shown in diagram. Glue in place.
- Position yellow butterfly wings and edges and glue in place.
- Position letters and glue in place.
- Glue small dots on butterfly and in other places as indicated, varying colors.
- Run thin lines of glue and press on black yarn between color changes in background, around each dot and butterfly.
- Slip rod into rod pocket and hang.

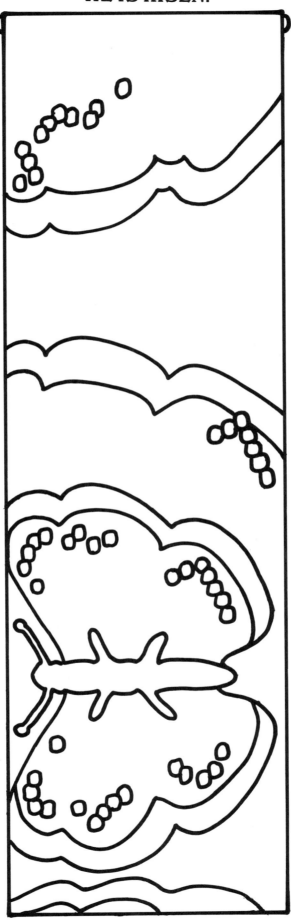

1" = 1'

SS2808

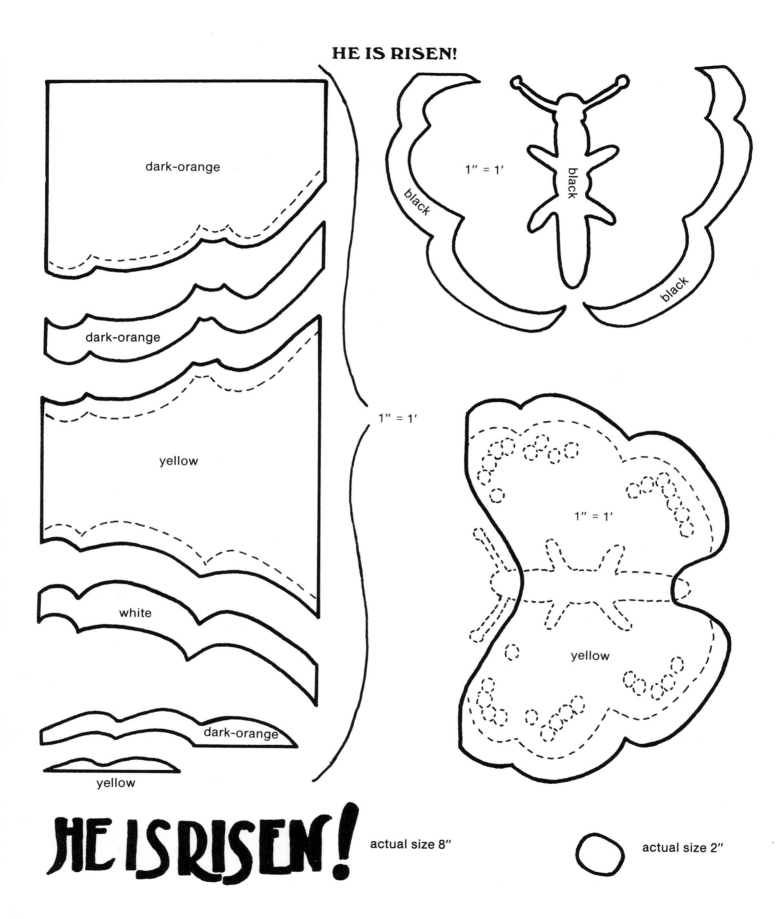

dark-orange

dark-orange

yellow

white

dark-orange

yellow

1" = 1'

black

black

black

1" = 1'

1" = 1'

yellow

HE IS RISEN!

actual size 8"

actual size 2"

# HE IS RISEN!

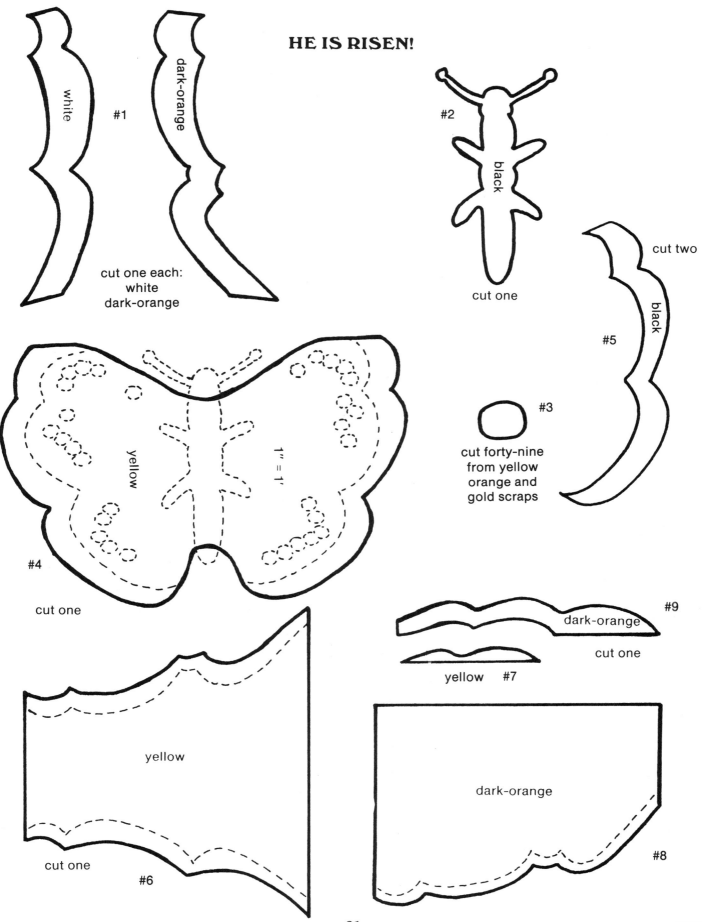

white #1

dark-orange

cut one each:
white
dark-orange

#2 black

cut one

cut two

black

#5

#3

cut forty-nine
from yellow
orange and
gold scraps

yellow

1" = 1'

#4

cut one

#9

dark-orange

cut one

yellow #7

yellow

dark-orange

cut one

#6

#8

SS2808

# HALLELUJAH! KING OF KINGS, HE SHALL REIGN FOREVER
## BASED ON REVELATION 19:6

Suggested size 3' x 9'

MATERIALS:

Basic supplies (see introduction)
3' x 10' red burlap
3 yards white felt
25 yards red yarn
Silver glitter (optional)

INSTRUCTIONS:

- Prepare background burlap by running a zigzag of glue around edges to prevent fraying.
- Pull thread 6" from top and bottom to form hemline and rod pocket.
- Turn hem and rod pocket to back and glue close to edge.
- Enlarge patterns using opaque projector or copier.
- Cut all letters, exclamation point, and crown piece #'s 2-6 from white felt (note that crown is made from 3 exclamation points).
- Cut word frame pieces from white felt, piecing where necessary.
- Place frame pieces for words on red background. Arrange letters according to design.
- Glue circle of red yarn about ½" from outer edge and on circles at base of exclamation points and crown piece #5.
- (Optional) Spread glue inside red yarn circle and sprinkle glitter on each circle.
- (Optional) Spread glue inside center of the a's in *hallelujah* and sprinkle glitter on each.
- Run thread of glue inside red yarn on each circle and in centers of a's in *hallelujah* to form stars. Press red yarn on glue.
- Run glue to form pointed accents and double lines on exclamation point and crown. Press red yarn on glue.
- Run wavy line of glue on crown base #6 and press red yarn on glue.
- Squeeze long lines of glue onto burlap to form starburst from upper left corner. Press red yarn onto glue, carefully gluing ends where they meet felt pieces.
- Slip rod into rod pocket and hang.

SS2808

## HALLELUJAH! KING OF KINGS, HE SHALL REIGN FOREVER

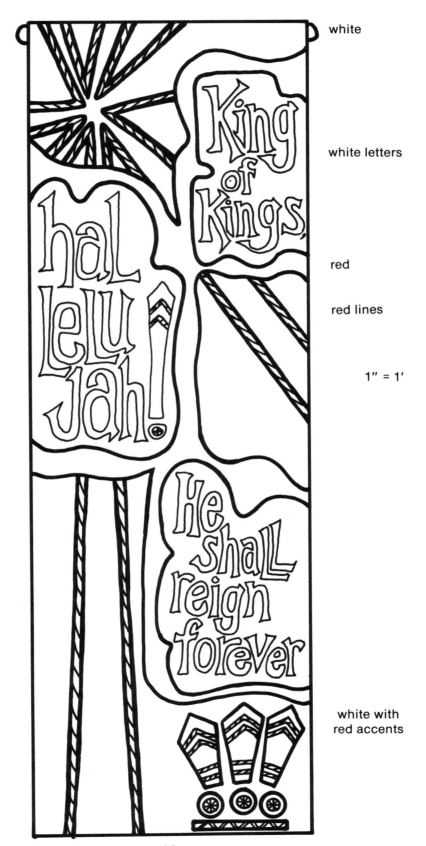

white

white letters

red

red lines

1" = 1'

white with
red accents

SS2808

# HALLELUJAH! KING OF KINGS HE SHALL REIGN FOREVER

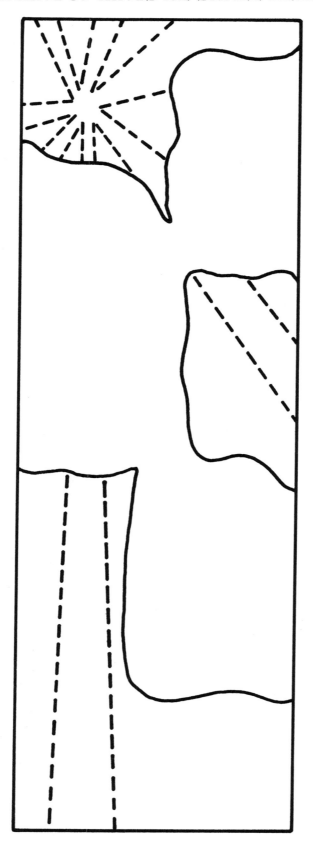

Starburst guides for red yarn lines.

1″ = 1′

SS2808

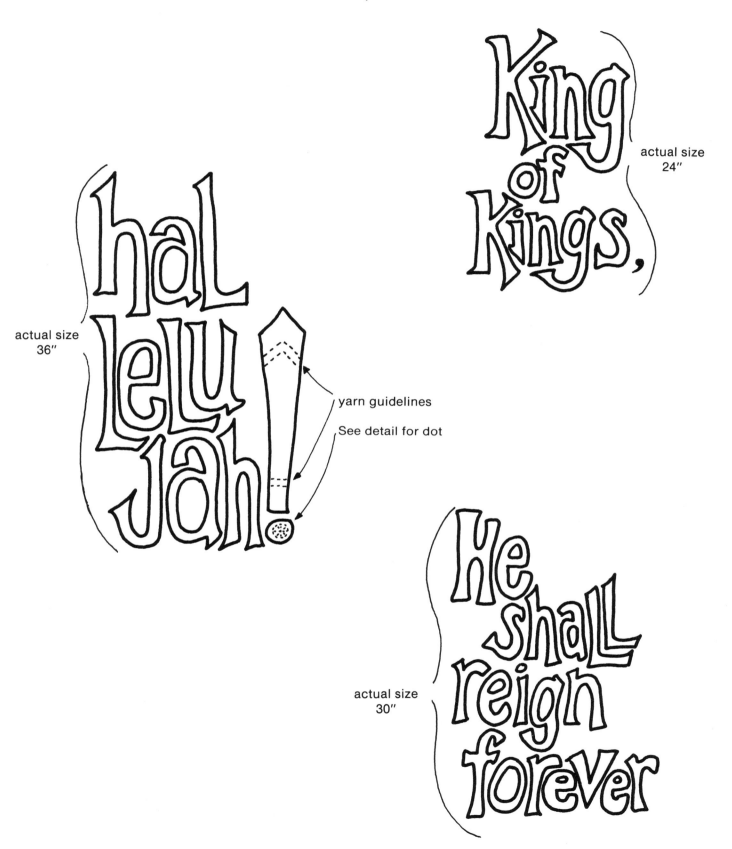

actual size 24"

actual size 36"

yarn guidelines

See detail for dot

actual size 30"

SS2808

# HALLELUJAH! KING OF KINGS, HE SHALL REIGN FOREVER

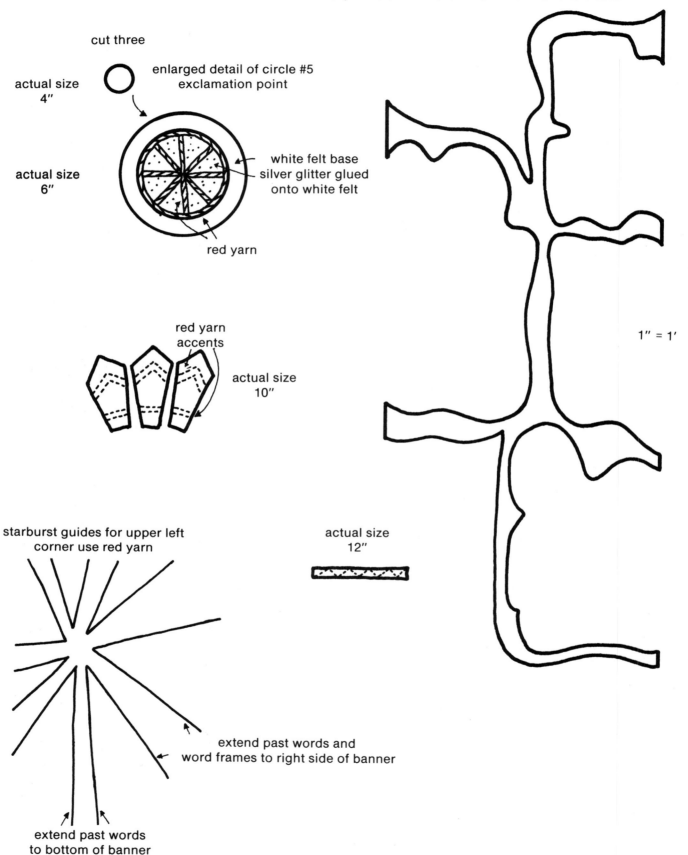

cut three

actual size
4"

enlarged detail of circle #5
exclamation point

actual size
6"

white felt base
silver glitter glued
onto white felt

red yarn

red yarn
accents

actual size
10"

1" = 1'

starburst guides for upper left
corner use red yarn

actual size
12"

extend past words and
word frames to right side of banner

extend past words
to bottom of banner

SS2808

# CHRIST IS RISEN, ALLELUIA!

## BASED ON LUKE 24:6

Suggested size 3' x 9'
MATERIALS:
Basic supplies (see introduction)
3' x 10' white burlap
3' x 9' white felt
¾ yard red felt
8 yards red yarn
INSTRUCTIONS:
- Prepare white burlap by running a zigzag of glue around the edges to prevent fraying.
- Pull a thread 6" from the top and bottom edge to form hemlines but do not turn hems back.
- Enlarge patterns using opaque projector or copier.
- The large piece of white felt is glued onto the white burlap background after the symbols* have been cut out of the felt. The white burlap will show through.
- Leaving 8" at the top, carefully trace the symbol patterns onto the white felt. Use a sharp felt tip marker or any pen that will not bleed. Note how the symbols are arranged in rows and how the pattern shifts. Be sure to keep lines straight.
- Cut the symbols out of the white felt, carefully cutting away any markings.
- Lay the cut piece of white felt on top of the white burlap background. Glue in place. Glue diamond-shaped pieces of white on the center peak of each crown and a narrow strip of white felt across middle of each crown as shown.
- Run a thread of glue around outines of symbols in second row from the bottom. Press red yarn in glue.
- Cut letters out of red felt and position. Glue in place.
- Fold hems to back and glue.
- Slide rod into rod pocket and hang.

\* The Chi-Rho consists of the first two letters of the Greek word for Christ. The empty cross is the symbol for Christ's victorious sacrifice—the symbol of our salvation. God is eternal—these letters, the Alpha and Omega are the first and last letters in the Greek alphabet. Christ is the beginning and the ending. The crown symbolizes the kingship of Christ as He reigns now and forever.

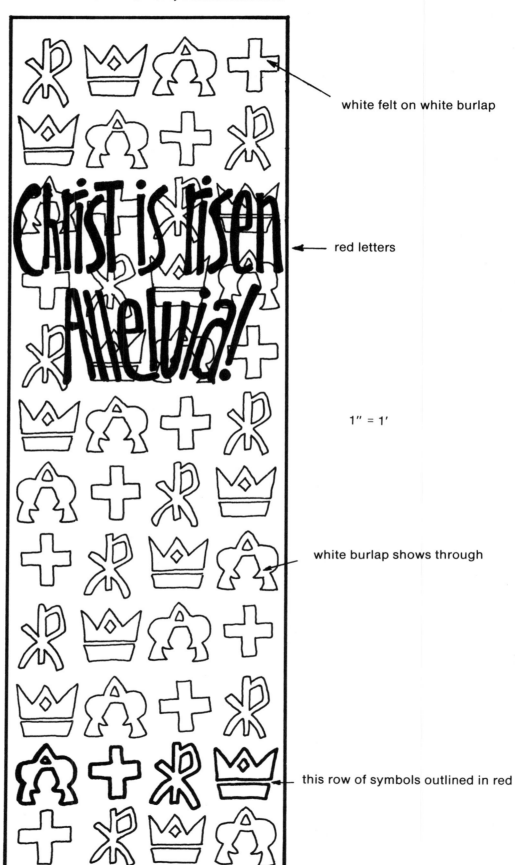

white felt on white burlap

red letters

1″ = 1′

white burlap shows through

this row of symbols outlined in red

# CHRIST IS RISEN, ALLELUIA!

actual size
7"

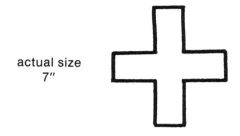

actual size
7"

actual size
7"

actual size
7"

SS2808

# CHRIST IS RISEN, ALLELUIA!

actual size
28"

# HE IS NOT HERE . . . HE IS RISEN! ALLELUIA! ALLELUIA!

## BASED ON LUKE 24:6

Suggested size 3' x 5½' each

MATERIALS:

Basic supplies (see introduction)
2 3½' x 6' pieces lavender felt
1 yard dark-lavender or purple felt
¼ yard each pink, white and green felt
35 feet white rug yarn

INSTRUCTIONS:

- Turn back 3" on long sides and glue close to edge.
- Turn back 3" on top and bottom for rod pockets. Glue close to edge.
- Enlarge designs using opaque projector or copier.
- Cut letters from dark-lavender.
- Cut leaves, stems, and vines from green felt.
- Cut flower petals from pink, dark-lavender and white felt. (Flower petals are all basically one shape with a few variations, so cut lots of the basic shape and adjust a few others for variety.)
- Arrange letters on background as shown.
- Glue green vines first, then flowers, working down and around garland.
- Add flower centers.
- Glue letters in place.
- Run a thread of glue 2" from edge all the way around the banner, interrupting if flower extends into edge. Press white rug yarn around edge to frame banners.
- Slip rods into rod pockets and hang.

purple letters

lavender background

white border line

1″ = 1′

1″ = 1′

flowers: pink
purple
white

green leaves and stems

# He is not here...
# He is
# Risen!

actual size
large letters-6"
small letters-4"

# Alleluia!
# Alleluia!

SS2808

# HE IS NOT HERE . . . HE IS RISEN! ALLELUIA! ALLELUIA!

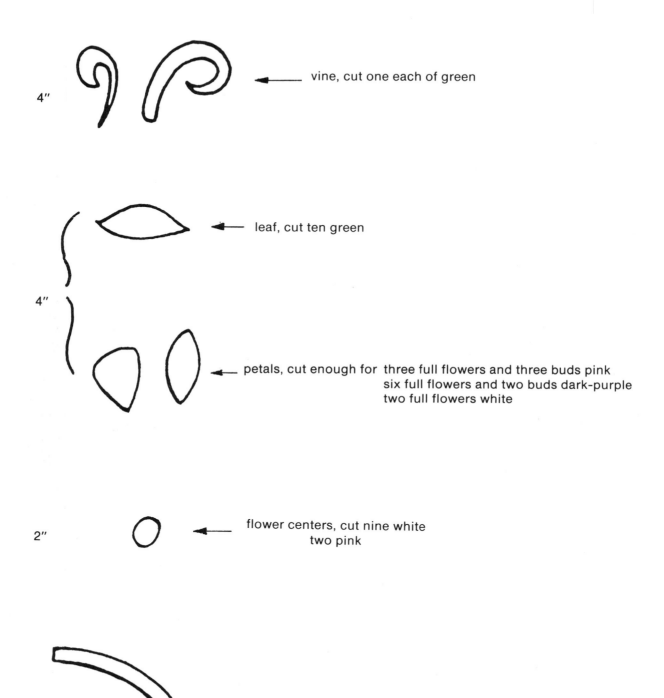

4″ — vine, cut one each of green

4″ — leaf, cut ten green

petals, cut enough for three full flowers and three buds pink
six full flowers and two buds dark-purple
two full flowers white

2″ — flower centers, cut nine white
two pink

8″ — stem, cut twelve green

SS2808

# BLESSED IS THE NATION WHOSE GOD IS THE LORD

## PSALM 33:12

Suggested size 3' x 7'

MATERIALS:

Basic supplies (see introduction)
3' x 8' medium-blue burlap
1 yard white felt
½ yard red felt

INSTRUCTIONS:

- Prepare background by running a zigzag of glue around edges to prevent fraying.
- Pull thread 6" from the top and bottom to form hemlines and rod pockets.
- Turn hems to back, glue close to edge.
- Enlarge patterns using opaque projector or copier.
- Cut red felt stripes—2 24" x 1" and 2 66" x 1". Piece if necessary.
- Cut white felt stripes—2 24" x ½" and 2 66" x ½". Piece if necessary.
- Cut letters from white felt and place on background.
- Cut four stars from white felt and place in corners.
- Position red stripes, centering between stars.
- Place white stripes on outside of red stripes.
- Glue all letters, stars and color stripes.
- Slide rods into rod pockets and hang.

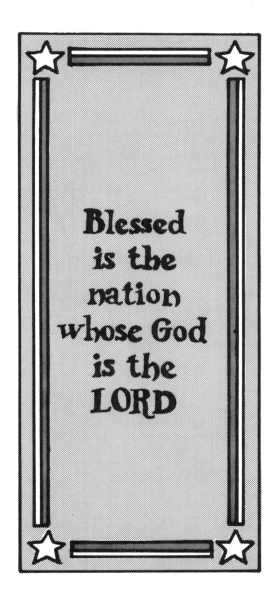

# BLESSED IS THE NATION WHOSE GOD IS THE LORD

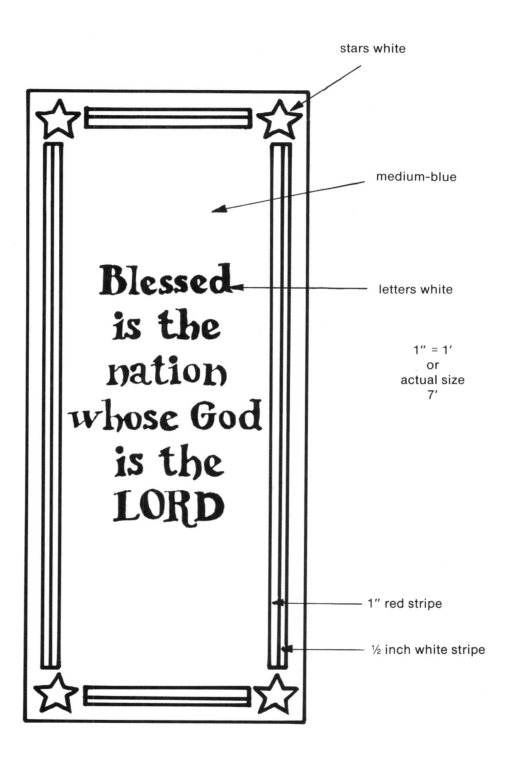

stars white

medium-blue

letters white

1" = 1'
or
actual size
7'

1" red stripe

½ inch white stripe

36

SS2808

# BLESSED IS THE NATION WHOSE GOD IS THE LORD

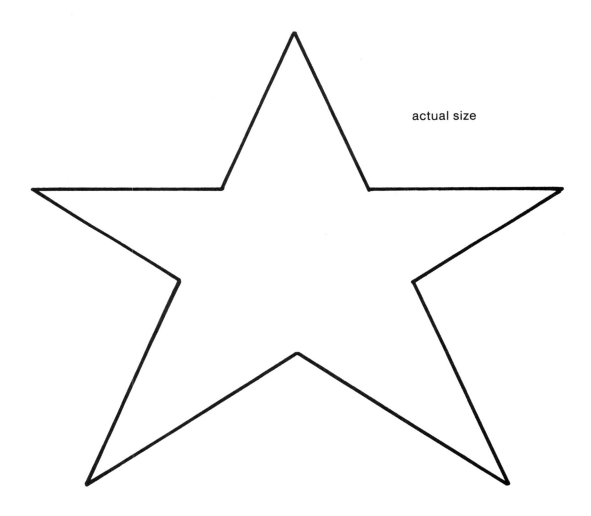

actual size

SS2808

cut four stars from white felt

# Blessed is the nation whose God is the LORD

actual size 4"

cut letters from white felt

SS2808

# CHRIST, THE LIGHT OF THE WORLD
## BASED ON JOHN 8:12

Suggested size 3' x 9'

MATERIALS:

Basic supplies (see introduction)
3' x 9½' dark-purple felt
2 yards light-purple felt
1½ yards white felt
4 yards white rug yarn

INSTRUCTIONS:

- Prepare dark-purple background piece by folding back 6" hem at top. Glue or sew hem in place.
- Enlarge patterns on opaque projector or copier.
- Cut out bottom edge arches according to pattern #5.
- Cut away inside of 4 diamonds #'s 4, 5, 6 and 7 at bottom.
- Cut 2" edging for long sides of banner, bottom arches, flames #3 and top flame #4 from light-purple felt. Piece if necessary.
- Cut out letters and top flame #1 from white felt.
- Glue light purple edge and shape #3 and #4 in place.
- Glue letters in place.
- Run thread of glue around each diamond opening on bottom edge and along flames at bottom. Press white yarn along glue.
- Slide rod into rod pocket and hang.

## CHRIST, THE LIGHT OF THE WORLD

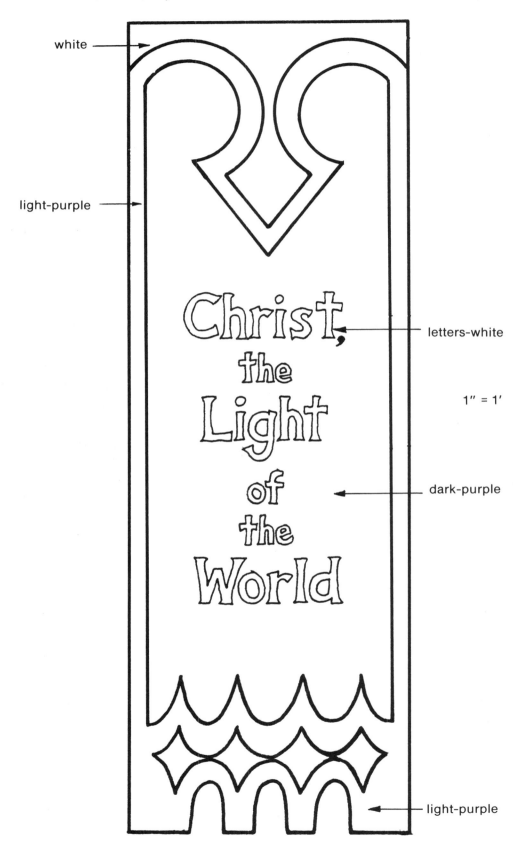

white

light-purple

Christ,
the
Light
of
the
World

letters-white

1″ = 1′

dark-purple

light-purple

SS2808

# CHRIST, THE LIGHT OF THE WORLD

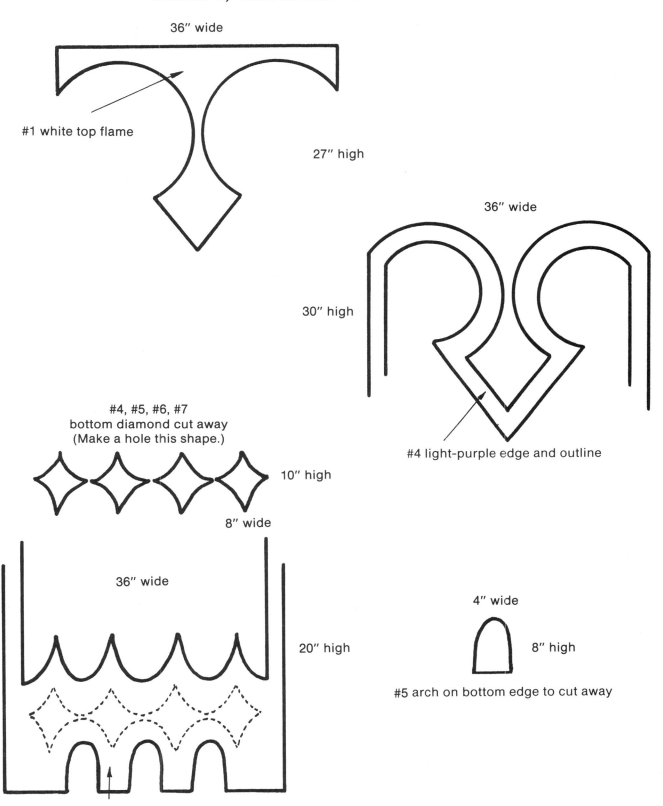

36" wide

27" high

#1 white top flame

36" wide

30" high

#4 light-purple edge and outline

#4, #5, #6, #7
bottom diamond cut away
(Make a hole this shape.)

10" high

8" wide

36" wide

20" high

#3 light-purple edge and outline

4" wide

8" high

#5 arch on bottom edge to cut away

Shining Star Publications, Copyright © 1992, A Division of Good Apple

SS2808

# Christ, the Light of the World

actual size
4"
large letters-4"
small letters-3"

Shining Star Publications, Copyright © 1992, A Division of Good Apple

SS2808

# THE WORD WAS MADE FLESH AND DWELT AMONG US

## BASED ON JOHN 1:14 KJV

Suggested size 3' x 8'

MATERIALS:

Basic supplies (see introduction)
3' x 9' white burlap
1½ yards light/natural burlap
½ yard red felt
½ yard brown or dark tan felt or burlap
7 yards brown yarn

INSTRUCTIONS:

- Prepare white background by running a zigzag of glue along edges to prevent fraying.
- Pull a thread 6" from the top and bottom edges to form hemlines. Turn hems to back along line; glue close to edge. This forms top rod pocket and bottom hem.
- Enlarge patterns using opaque projector or copier.
- Cut cross from red felt; piece if necessary.
- Cut letters from red felt.
- Cut hand patterns from natural burlap as shown.
- Cut shading pieces for hand from brown felt as shown.
- Position hand piece #'s 1-6 and letters as shown. Glue letters and main hand pieces in place.
- Position shading pieces and glue in place.
- Run thread of glue around outside of each piece of hand and press yarn on as outline.
- Position cross on top of hand; glue in place.
- Run rod through rod pocket and hang.

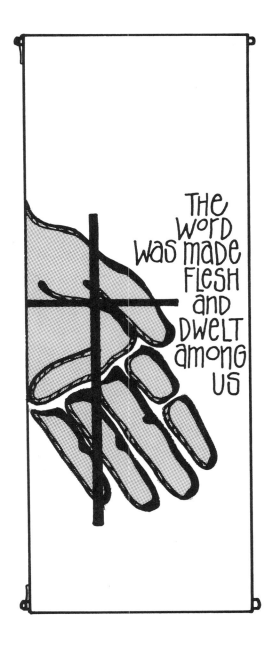

SS2808

# THE WORD WAS MADE FLESH AND DWELT AMONG US

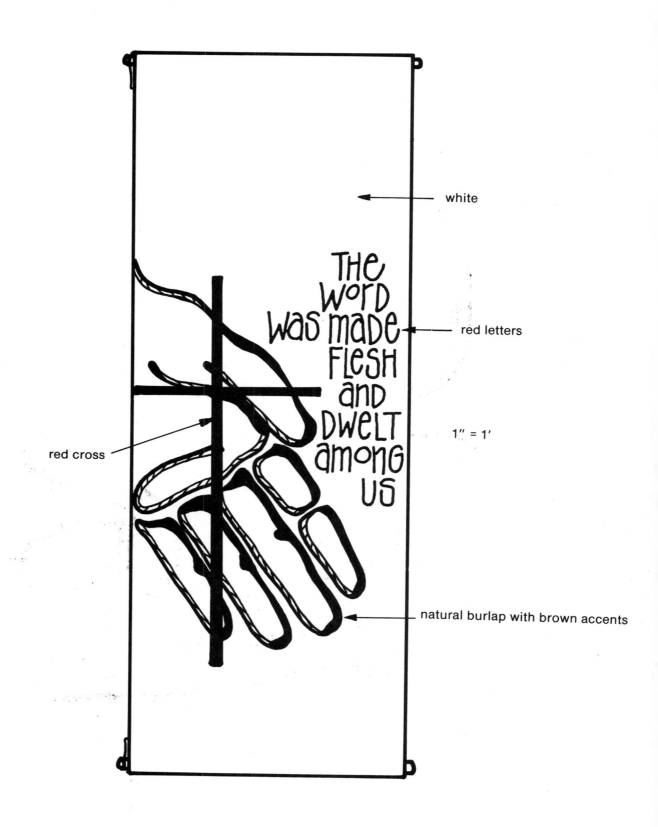

white

red letters

red cross

1″ = 1′

natural burlap with brown accents

# THE WORD WAS MADE FLESH AND DWELT AMONG US

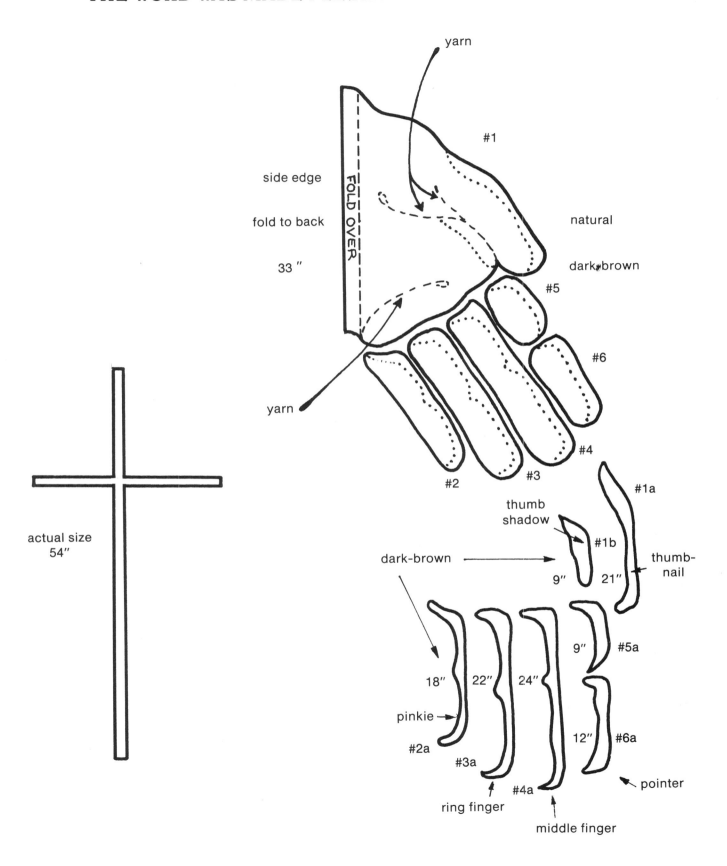

actual size
54"

yarn

side edge

fold to back

33 "

FOLD OVER

#1

natural

dark-brown

#5

#6

#4

#3

#2

yarn

#1a

thumb
shadow

#1b

thumb-
nail

9"

21"

dark-brown

9"

#5a

18"

22"

24"

pinkie

#2a

#3a

ring finger

#4a

middle finger

12"

#6a

pointer

SS2808

actual size
4"

# PEACE ON EARTH

## BASED ON LUKE 2:14

Suggested size 3' x 9'

MATERIALS:

Basic supplies (see introduction)
3' x 9½' natural burlap
2 yards white felt
⅛ yard per child appropriate flesh colors
felt and fabric scraps in the following
    colors: navy, black, white, brown, red,
    gold, yellow, denim, floral.
Yarn and ribbon

INSTRUCTIONS:

- Prepare background burlap by running a zigzag of glue along edges to prevent fraying.
- Pull a thread 6" from top to mark hemline, fold to wrong side and glue near edge for rod pocket.
- Fray bottom by pulling threads for approximately 4". Glue on wrong side at top of fringe to prevent further fraying.
- Enlarge patterns using opaque projector or copier.
- Cut English words from red felt.
- Cut other language words from white felt.
- Cut six children's bodies from appropriate flesh colors.
- Cut clothing, hair, facial features, hands and feet from various colors of fabric.
- Arrange white letters on background as shown using threads of burlap to keep the lines straight.
- Arrange flesh cutouts of children as shown. Be sure hands touch. Glue in place.
- Center red letters beneath cutouts. Glue in place.
- Add clothing, hair and features to each body.
- Run rod through rod pocket and hang.

संसार में शान्ति

平和어 地上에

平
安

שלום

1″ = 1′

SS2808

# PEACE ON EARTH

SS2808

# PEACE ON EARTH

for facial features, use scraps of blue, brown, pink and red

size of figure 18″

**Netherlands**
- yellow hair
- tie
- coat
- pants
- shoes

**Philippines**
- black hair
- shirt
- pants
- bare feet

**India**
- black hair
- dress
- sandals
- stripe

**United States**
- brown/black hair
- shirt
- blue jeans
- tennis shoes

**Sweden**
- yellow hair
- blouse
- vest with lace
- skirt apron
- clogs

**Korea**
- black hair
- shirt
- tie
- skirt
- leggings
- shoes

50

SS2808

# PEACE ON EARTH

Friede auf Erden — Germany

संसार में शान्ति — India

SíOCHAN AR DOMHAIN — Ireland

Pace sul Terra — Italy

平和 여 地上 에) — Korea

all letters 6"

HA ЗЕМЛЕ МИР — Russia

Paz en la Tierra — France

VREDE OP AARDE — Netherlands

FRED PÅ JORDEN — Sweden

PEACE ON EARTH — United States

שלום — Greece

平安 — China

Kapayapaan sa Lupa — Philippines

SS2808

# JOY
## BASED ON LUKE 2:10

Suggested size: 3' x 7½'

MATERIALS:

Basic supplies (see introduction)
3' x 9' red burlap
2½' x 3' red-print fabric (bold print without much white)
2½' x 3½' white felt
30' thick green yarn
Blue felt
Cardboard
2 large red ornaments
2 large pinecones

INSTRUCTIONS:

- Run zigzag of glue along sides of burlap to prevent fraying.
- Pull thread 15" from top hem to form hemline. Fold and pin; do not glue.
- Cut rectangles out of top hem 12" x 8".
- Open out hem and glue all edges of rectangles to prevent raveling. Allow glue to dry.
- Fold hem to wrong side. Glue a line 12" from top and a line 15" from top to form the rod pocket.
- Enlarge patterns using opaque projector or copier.
- Cut red-print fabric according to pattern.
- Glue print on red burlap background as shown.
- Cut letters out of white felt.
- Place letters on red print and glue.
- Cut lengths of thick red yarn: 2-4½'; 2-3¾'; 1-3½'.
- Attach yarn 1" below red print pattern as shown. Glue securely or sew.
- Make Star of David by cutting the shape from cardboard. Glue blue felt onto shape.
- Glue ornaments, pinecones and Star of David to ends of red yarn. Attach to bottom of banner being sure items dangle to the same length.
- Insert rods and hang.

1″ = 1′
or
actual size
7½′

# JOY

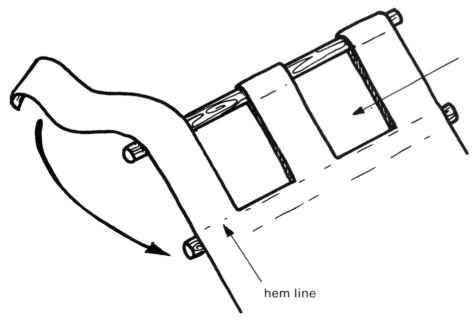

shape to cut away from hem after folding

actual size
8″ wide and 12″ high

hem line

actual size
3″

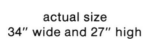

actual size
34″ wide and 27″ high

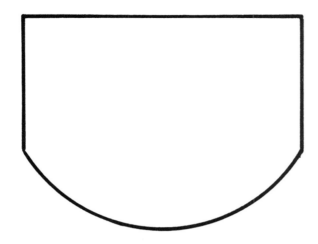

red-print fabric

cut from cardboard and cover with blue felt

white felt

actual size
24"

# DEAD TO SIN—ALIVE IN CHRIST
## BASED ON JOHN 5:25

Suggested size: 1½' x 5' each

MATERIALS:

Basic supplies (see introduction)
2 22" x 5½' pieces pale-blue burlap
4 18" x 16" pieces of blue felt in 4 different shades
2 18" x 12" pieces blue-green felt
¼ yard very dark-blue felt
Yarn scraps, shades of blue and white

INSTRUCTIONS:

- Prepare background pieces by turning 2" on long sides to back; glue along edges.
- Pull thread 3" from top and bottom for hemlines. Turn to wrong side and glue along edge.
- Enlarge patterns using opaque projector or copier.
- Cut letters from dark-blue felt.
- Cut piece #'s 1-4, one from each shade of blue; repeat with #'s 6-9.
- Cut piece #'s 5 and 10 from blue-green. Fold under at dotted line and glue to wrong side.
- Place all water pieces on background as shown. Glue.
- Place all letters on background and glue.
- Slip rods into rod pockets and hang.

1″ = 1′

SS2808

# DEAD TO SIN—ALIVE IN CHRIST

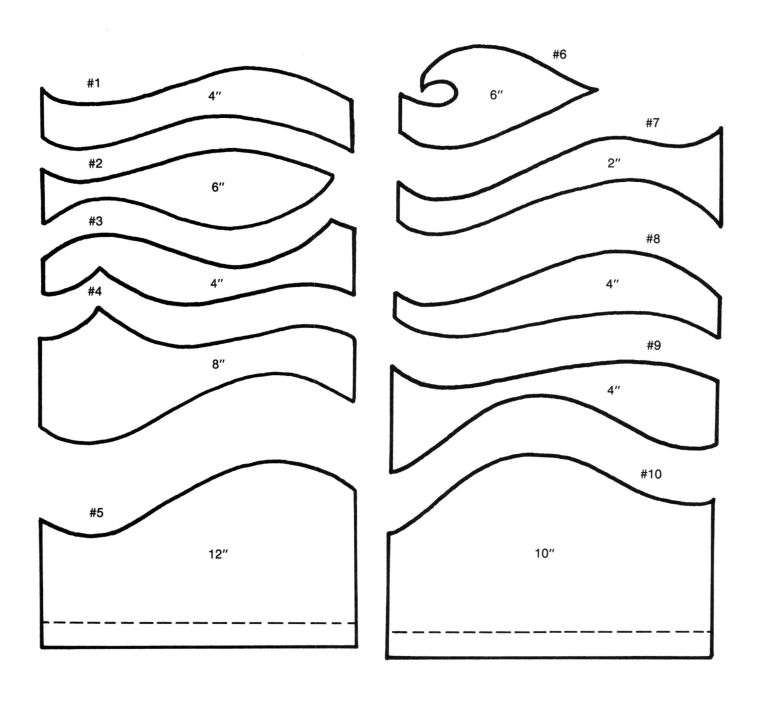

#1  4"

#2  6"

#3  4"

#4  8"

#5  12"

#6  6"

#7  2"

#8  4"

#9  4"

#10  10"

waves various shades of blue

#5 and #10 green for bottom pieces

SS2808

letters dark-blue

actual size
small letters-2″
large letters-4″

# dead to sin

# alive in Christ

SS2808

**MARRIAGE**

# TWO SHALL BECOME ONE

## BASED ON GENESIS 2:24

Suggested size: 2½' x 9'

MATERIALS:

Basic supplies (see introduction)
2½' x 10' white felt
½ yard medium-blue felt
⅛ yard light-blue felt
⅛ yard dark-blue felt
10 yards medium-blue yarn
⅛ yard yellow felt
Note: This can be made in a color scheme
to match the wedding colors.

INSTRUCTIONS:

- Measure 6" from top and bottom to make hemlines. Fold and glue hems in place.
- Enlarge patterns using opaque projector or copier.
- Cut letters from medium-blue felt and place on background.
- Cut lamp pattern from light-blue felt and place on background. Cut triangle overlap for lamps from dark-blue felt. Cut flames from yellow felt. Position all pieces on background.
- Make dove by running a thread of glue in the shape of a dove and pressing on yarn to form the outline. Run another thread of glue ½" outside of first outline and press on another length of yarn.
- Glue letters and lamp in place. Run thread of glue ½" around outside of lamp even with dark-blue triangle overlap piece. Press yarn onto glue.
- Glue yellow flame in place.
- Slide rod through rod pocket and hang.

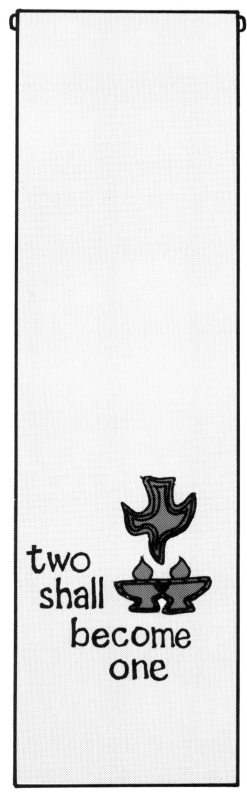

SS2808

# TWO SHALL BECOME ONE

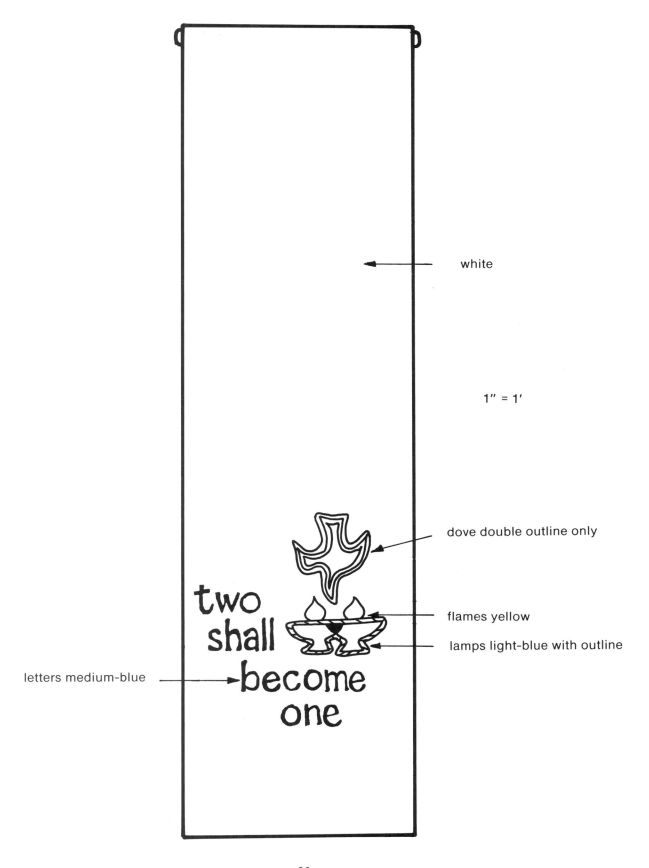

white

1″ = 1′

dove double outline only

flames yellow

lamps light-blue with outline

two shall become one

letters medium-blue

SS2808

# TWO SHALL BECOME ONE

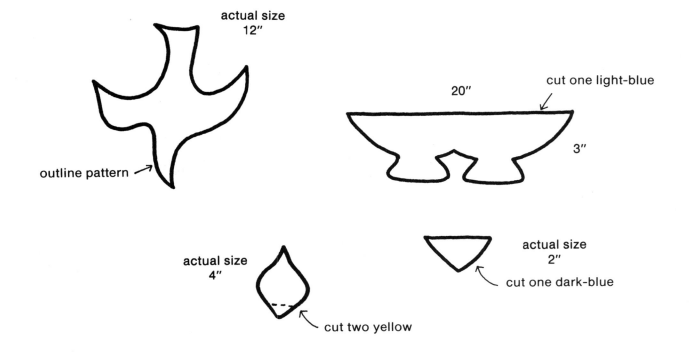

actual size
12"

cut one light-blue

20"

3"

outline pattern

actual size
2"

cut one dark-blue

actual size
4"

cut two yellow

# two shall become one

actual size
4″

letters medium-blue

SS2808

# LET US MAKE A COVENANT TOGETHER YOU AND I

### BASED ON LUKE 22:20

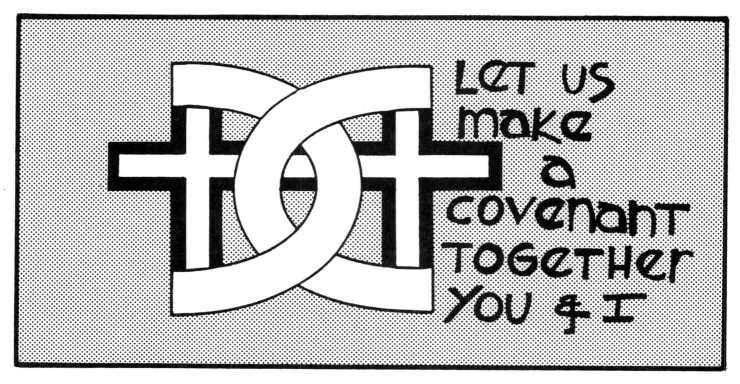

Suggested size: 5' x 2½'

MATERIALS:

Basic supplies (see introduction)
5½' x 3' natural tan burlap
24" x 24" white felt
36" x 24" rose felt
3 yards rose yarn
Note: This can be made in a color scheme to match the wedding colors.

INSTRUCTIONS:
- Prepare background burlap by turning 3" on long sides to back; glue along edges.
- Pull a thread 3" from top and bottom for hemlines. Turn hems and glue at edge. This forms top rod pocket and bottom hem.
- Enlarge patterns using opaque projector or copier.
- Cut letters from rose felt.
- Cut background cross from rose felt.
- Cut inside crosses and arcs from white felt.
- Place rose crosses and letters on background using threads of burlap as guide for straightness. Glue in place.
- Center white inside crosses on top of background crosses. Glue in place.
- Place white arcs in place and glue. Note how they entwine.
- Run a thread of glue around all edges of arcs. Press yarn along glued edge, clipping where one arc goes behind the other. Be sure ends of yarn are securely glued.
- Slide rod into rod pocket and hang.

# LET US MAKE A COVENANT TOGETHER YOU AND I

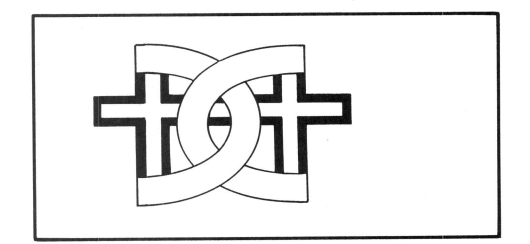

1″ = 1′

# LET US MAKE A COVENANT TOGETHER YOU AND I

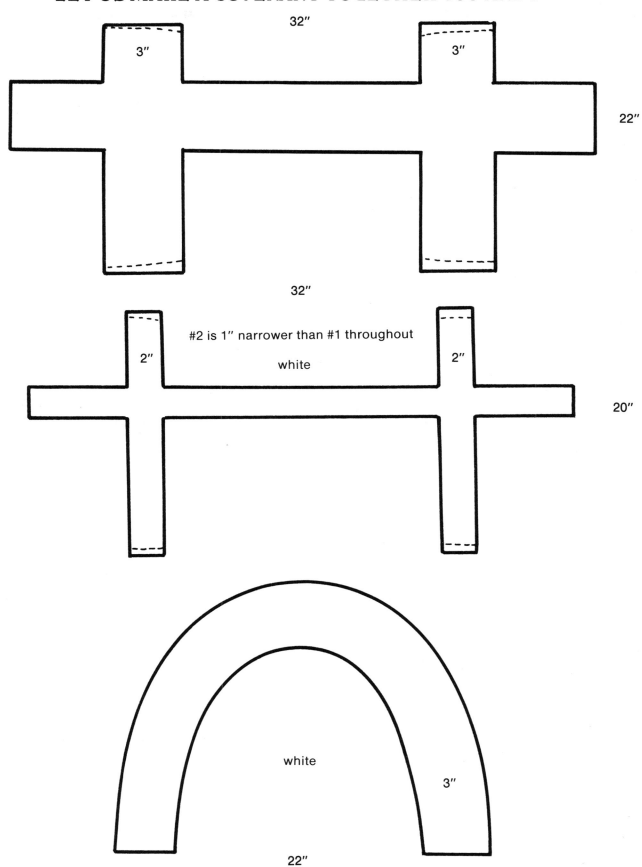

32"

3"

3"

22"

32"

2"

#2 is 1" narrower than #1 throughout

white

2"

20"

white

3"

22"

# LET US MAKE A COVENANT TOGETHER YOU AND I

LET US
make
a
covenant
TOGETHER
YOU & I

actual size
4″

# SING, SING, SING FOR JOY!

## BASED ON PSALM 95:1

Suggested size: 3' x 9'

MATERIALS:

Basic supplies (see introduction)
3' x 5'8" natural burlap
1  3' x 2'1" piece of red burlap
1  3' x 2'7" piece of red burlap
⅛ yard felt of each: bright-goldenrod, bright-blue, orange, red, light-green
Scraps of bright felt colors

INSTRUCTIONS:

- Prepare background by running a zigzag of glue along edges to prevent fraying.
- To make background piece, sew or glue red burlap to natural burlap, with the 2'1" piece at top and 2'7" piece at bottom.
- Pull thread 6" from top and bottom to make hemlines. Turn hems to wrong side and glue near edge. This forms the rod pocket.
- Enlarge patterns using opaque projector or copier.
- Cut one *sing* from orange felt, one from light-green, one from red.
- Cut *for* from bright-blue felt.
- Cut *joy* from bright-goldenrod felt.
- Cut 40 circles from many different colors of felt.
- Cut 40 hearts from many different colors of felt.
- Cut 30 crosses from many different colors of felt.
- Position words on center natural section.
- Rows of crosses, circles and hearts cover both top and bottom seams. Top row of crosses begins on seam line and arches above seam. Place circles and hearts in rows beneath crosses. Mix colors.
- On bottom rows, circles begin just above seam line, dip and come back to just above seam line. Hearts are placed above circles, crosses below. Mix colors.
- Glue on all letters, hearts, circles, and crosses.
- Slip rod into rod pocket and hang.

# SING, SING, SING FOR JOY!

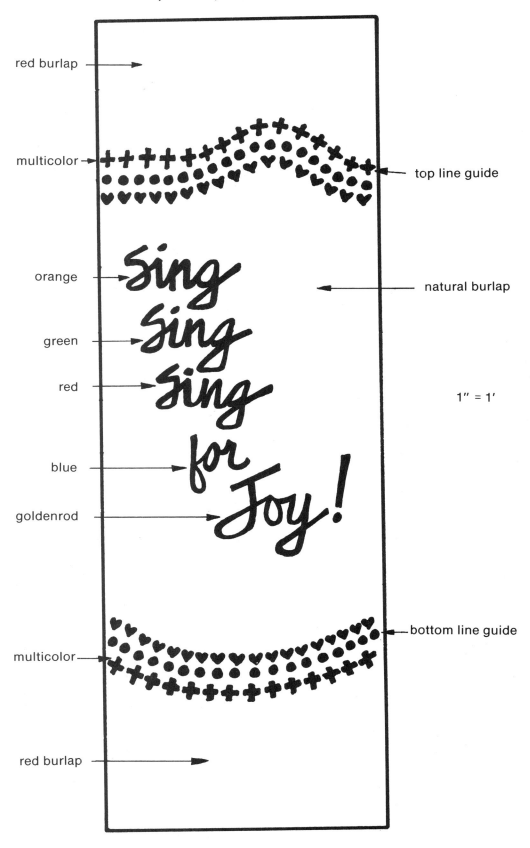

1" = 1'

SS2808

# SING, SING, SING FOR JOY!

actual size
2"

70

SS2808

cut three different colors

actual size
10"

cut one

cut one

# AS FOR ME AND MY HOUSE, WE WILL SERVE THE LORD
## BASED ON JOSHUA 24:15

Suggested size: 3' x 9'

MATERIALS:

Basic supplies (see introduction)
3' x 10' yellow burlap
3' x 14" light-orange felt or burlap
3' x 12" medium-blue felt or burlap
50" x 24" tan felt or burlap
6" x 10" each red and yellow felt
1 yard dark-blue felt

INSTRUCTIONS:

- Prepare yellow background by running a zigzag of glue along edges to prevent raveling.
- Pull a thread 6" from top and bottom to mark hemlines. Fold to back and glue close to edge.
- Enlarge patterns using opaque projector or copier.
- Arrange large color pieces on yellow background. Glue.
- Arrange words on yellow, using burlap threads as a guide for straightness.
- Arrange tan houses on and glue.
- For special house, glue yellow pieces to the wrong side of red and blue as if light were coming out of the openings. Turn to right side.
- Glue houses and words in place.
- Glue red heart above door of special house.
- Slip rod through rod pocket and hang.

Note: This design could be made into a two-banner set by duplicating the same house motifs in reverse and splitting the verse: As for Me and My House/We Will Serve the Lord. Use only one special house.

1" = 1'

# AS FOR ME AND MY HOUSE WE WILL SERVE THE LORD

actual size

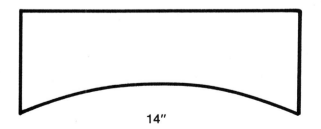

cut one light-orange

14"

12"

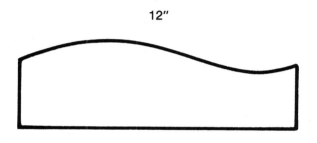

cut one medium-blue

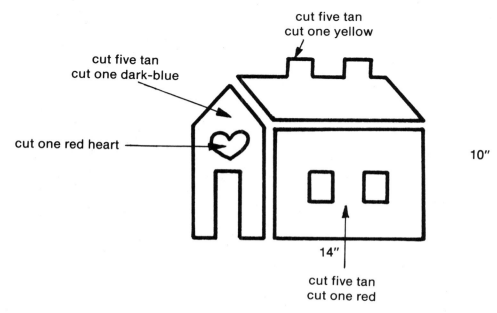

cut five tan
cut one yellow

cut five tan
cut one dark-blue

cut one red heart

10"

14"

cut five tan
cut one red

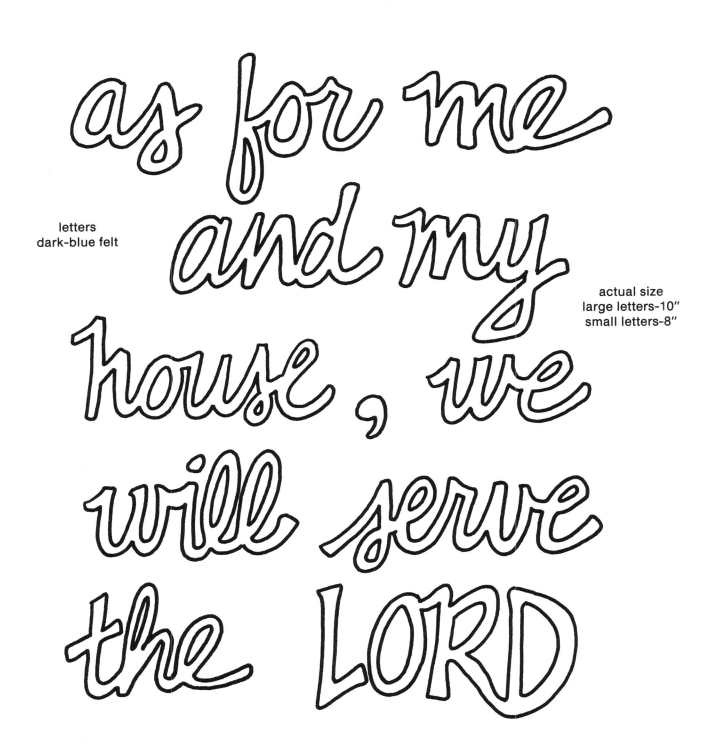

letters
dark-blue felt

actual size
large letters-10″
small letters-8″

# THANKS BE TO GOD
# WHO GIVES US THE VICTORY
# THROUGH OUR LORD JESUS CHRIST

### BASED ON I CORINTHIANS 15:57

Suggested size: 3′ x 10′

MATERIALS:

Basic supplies (see introduction)
3′ x 6′ green burlap
3′ x 6′ white burlap
3′ x 1½′ purple felt or burlap
3′ x 1½′ red felt or burlap
3′ x 1½′ black felt or burlap
¼ yard green felt
½ yard red felt

INSTRUCTIONS:

- Prepare edges of green burlap and white burlap by running a zigzag of glue along edges to prevent fraying.
- Glue green and white burlap together to make one long background piece 3′ x 11′.
- Pull a thread 6″ from top and bottom to form hemlines. Fold and glue edge.
- Enlarge patterns using opaque projector or copier.
- Cut piece #1 purple; cut piece #2 red; cut piece #3 black. Cut 15 leaves from green felt.
- Cut all letters out of red felt.
- Place pieces on background as shown in diagram and glue.
- Position green leaves and glue.
- Position letters and glue.
- Slip rod through rod pocket and hang.

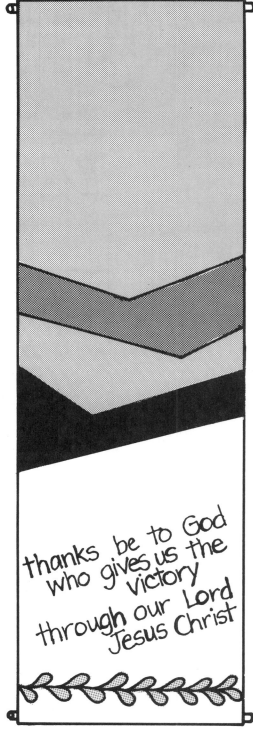

SS2808

# THANKS BE TO GOD WHO GIVES US THE VICTORY
## THROUGH OUR LORD JESUS CHRIST

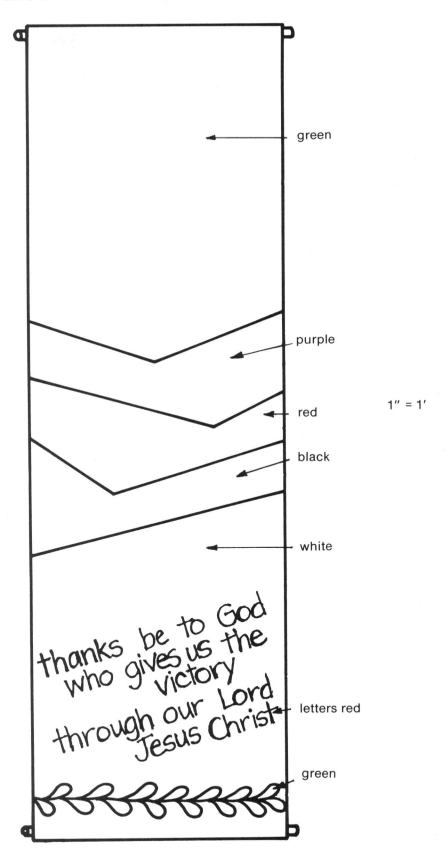

green

purple

red

1" = 1'

black

white

thanks be to God who gives us the victory through our Lord Jesus Christ

letters red

green

SS2808

# THANKS BE TO GOD WHO GIVES US THE VICTORY
# THROUGH OUR LORD JESUS CHRIST

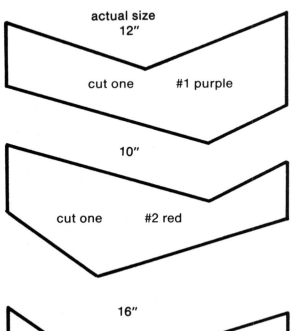

actual size
12"

cut one    #1 purple

10"

cut one    #2 red

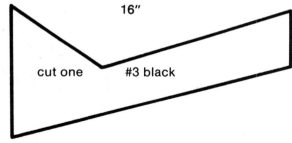

16"

cut one    #3 black

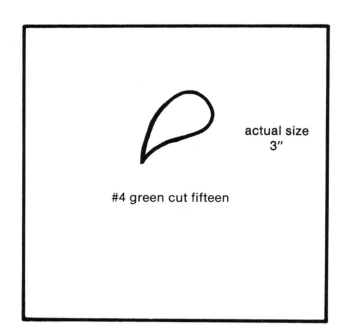

actual size
3"

#4 green cut fifteen

## THANKS BE TO GOD WHO GIVES US THE VICTORY
## THROUGH OUR LORD JESUS CHRIST

actual size
4″

letters red felt

thanks be to God who gives us the victory through our Lord Jesus Christ

SS2808

# LET US FIX OUR EYES ON JESUS

## BASED ON HEBREWS 12:2

Suggested size: 2½' x 5½'

MATERIALS:

Basic supplies (see introduction)
2½' x 6' royal blue burlap
1 yard bright-yellow felt
4 16" x 12" pieces blue felt; 4 shades of blue, navy progressing to light-blue
1 16" x 12" piece white felt

INSTRUCTIONS:

- Prepare sides and top of blue background by running a zigzag of glue along edges to prevent fraying.
- Unravel 2" at bottom.
- Run a zigzag of glue along top of fringe to prevent further fraying.
- Pull a thread 6" from the top edge. Fold and glue close to edge.
- Enlarge patterns using opaque projector or copier.
- Cut patterns of circles and letters from yellow felt.
- Cut patterns of runners from 4 shades of blue and one white.
- Position large yellow circle on background and glue.
- Position runners overlapping across circle (use burlap thread as guide for straightness). Glue runners in place.
- Run a thread of glue around outside and inside edges of yellow circle; press on blue yarn. Tuck the ends under the runners.
- Arrange letters and dots above and below runners as shown.
- Run a line of glue around dots. Press yarn around each dot.
- Slip rod through rod pocket and hang.

# LET US FIX OUR EYES ON JESUS

blue

actual size
5½'

blue

SS2808

# LET US FIX OUR EYES ON JESUS

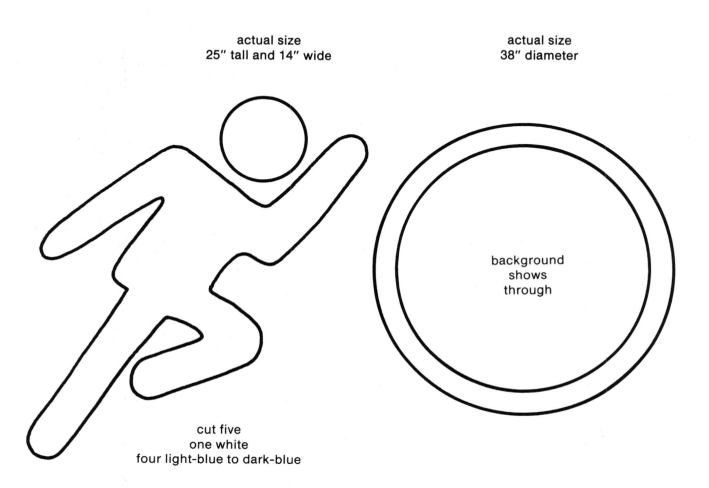

actual size
25" tall and 14" wide

actual size
38" diameter

background
shows
through

cut five
one white
four light-blue to dark-blue

SS2808

# LET US

cut all letters yellow

# FIX OUR EYES

# ON JESUS

actual size
4"

# • HEBREWS 12: 2 •

actual size
2½"

SS2808

# O MAGNIFY THE LORD WITH ME, LET US PRAISE HIS NAME TOGETHER!

## BASED ON PSALM 34:3

Suggested size: 3' x 9' each

## MATERIALS:

Basic supplies (see introduction)
2 3' x 10' pieces natural burlap
30" x 40" felt pieces, one each: gold, red, purple, white, yellow, green
6 10" x 10" felt pieces, one each: beige, white, brown, burgundy, black, yellow
2 yards red felt
½ yard white felt

## INSTRUCTIONS:

- Prepare natural background by running a zigzag of glue along edges to prevent raveling.
- Pull thread 6" from top and bottom to form hemlines.
- Fold hems to wrong side and glue.
- Enlarge patterns on opaque projector or copier. Make one pattern for #'s 2, 3 and 4 then flip the pattern pieces to make the mirror images #'s 2a, 3a, and 4a for the second banner.
- Cut all letters from red felt.
- Using the six body patterns, cut one of each color: gold, red, purple, white, yellow, green.
- Cut 1 head of each color: beige, white, brown, burgundy, black, yellow.
- Cut strips of white felt ½" wide for border. Cut enough strips to equal 50'.
- Place all worshipers on banners and carefully cut away any felt that is covered up by another piece. This will eliminate bumps on the figures.
- Glue bodies in place.
- Glue heads in place.
- Position letters and glue.
- Slip rods into rod pockets and hang.

SS2808

# O MAGNIFY THE LORD WITH ME, LET US PRAISE HIS NAME TOGETHER!

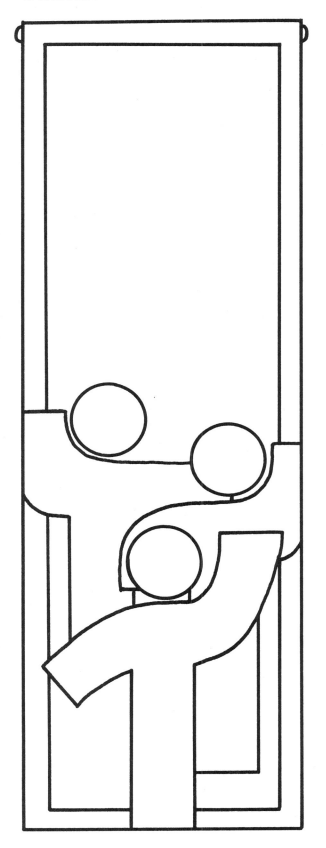

1″ = 1′

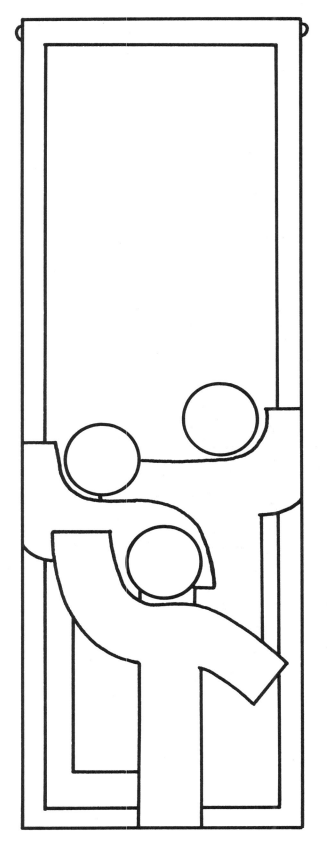

SS2808

# O MAGNIFY THE LORD WITH ME, LET US PRAISE HIS NAME TOGETHER!

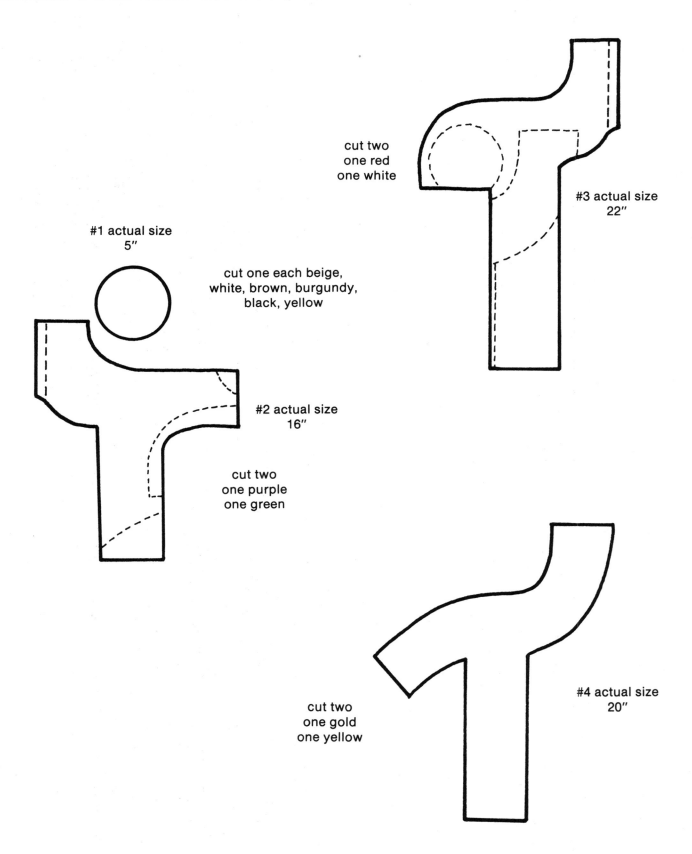

cut two
one red
one white

#3 actual size
22"

#1 actual size
5"

cut one each beige,
white, brown, burgundy,
black, yellow

#2 actual size
16"

cut two
one purple
one green

cut two
one gold
one yellow

#4 actual size
20"

SS2808

# O MAGNIFY THE LORD WITH ME, LET US PRAISE HIS NAME TOGETHER!

O magnify the Lord with me,

actual size
4"

all letters
red felt

Let us praise His name together!

# HOLY, HOLY, HOLY, THE WHOLE EARTH IS FILLED WITH HIS GLORY

## BASED ON ISAIAH 6:3

Suggested size: 27" x 30"

MATERIALS:

Basic supplies (see introduction)
27" x 33" brown burlap
Yellow, green, white, brown, pink and red felt scraps
¼ yard each of 3 shades of blue felt
Red, orange, yellow, green, blue, and purple yarn scraps
½ yard goldenrod felt

INSTRUCTIONS:

- Prepare brown burlap background by running a zigzag of glue along edges of top and sides.
- Measure 3" from top and pull one thread to mark hemline. Fold to wrong side and glue close to edge. This makes the rod pocket.
- Fray bottom edge approximately 1". Glue along top edge of fringe to prevent further fraying.
- Enlarge patterns on opaque projector or copier.
- Cut letters out of goldenrod felt and arrange as shown.
- Cut lengths of yarn to make rainbow and arrange under words. Position in order: red, orange, yellow, green, blue, purple.
- Cut tree trunk out of brown felt, large tree top of green and leaves from a different shade of green. Arrange under rainbow.
- Cut bear from dark brown felt. Use small dots of pink to accent ears and feet. Use red for nose and blue dots for eyes. Arrange under tree as shown.
- Cut small stripes of green for grass and arrange around bear.
- Cut flower from yellow, flower center from white. Use a narrow green stripe for a stem.
- Cut a large piece of light-blue for main water section #2. Cut other water patterns from shades of blue. Arrange inside words.
- Cut fish from dark-blue, duck from white, birds from blue and bubbles from light-blue. Cut small black dots for eyes.
- Glue all pieces in place.

background brown

actual size
30"

letters goldenrod

Shining Star Publications, Copyright © 1992, A Division of Good Apple

SS2808

# HOLY, HOLY, HOLY, THE WHOLE EARTH IS FILLED WITH HIS GLORY

cut eight leaves

½″    green

5″

yellow

1″

½″    green
white   1½

½″    eyes
nose   1″

7″    brown

¾″    grass

4″    brown

1″    cut two feet brown

9″

1″    blue

2″    white

¼″

1″    cut two fish
dark blue

2″

3″

shades of blue and green

1″

# HOLY, HOLY, HOLY, THE WHOLE EARTH IS FILLED WITH HIS GLORY

letters goldenrod

actual size
2″

cut three "HOLY"

# HOLY,+ THE WHOLE

# EARTH IS FILLED

# WITH HIS GLORY

SS2808

# GROW IN GRACE AND KNOWLEDGE OF OUR LORD AND SAVIOR JESUS CHRIST . . .

## II PETER 3:18

Suggested size: 3′ x 7′ each

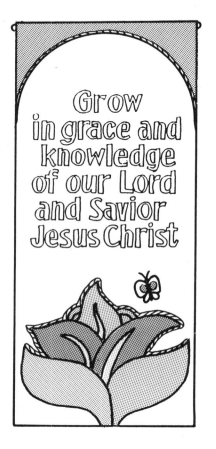

## MATERIALS:

Basic supplies (see introduction)
2  3′ x 7′8″ pieces dark-blue burlap
3 yards medium-green felt
1½ yards white felt
½ yard light-green felt
¼ yard red felt
15 yards olive green yarn
10 yards bright-yellow yarn
3 yards red yarn

## INSTRUCTIONS:

● Prepare dark-blue background pieces by running zigzag of glue along edges to prevent fraying.

● Pull thread 4″ from top and bottom edges to form hemlines. Turn hems to back and glue close to edge.

● Enlarge patterns using opaque projector or copier.

SS2808

# GROW IN GRACE AND KNOWLEDGE
## OF OUR LORD AND SAVIOR JESUS CHRIST . . .

Instructions (continued):

- Cut large leaves and stem pieces #1-10 from medium-green felt. Cut letters from white felt. Cut butterfly pieces as follows: #15 yellow, #16 and 17 white, #18 red, #19 yellow. Cut blossom #'s 11, 12, 13, 14 and 15 from white felt. Cut smaller blossom #'s 11a, 12a, 13a, 14a, 15a from red felt. Cut leaf accent #'s 3a, 4a, 5a, 7a, 8a, 9a, 10a from light-green felt. Cut arches #2 from white felt.
- Position Banner A leave #'s 1-5 according to design, folding back the bottoms of #'s 1 and 2 to wrong side. Glue. Add light-green accent #'s 3a-5a and glue. Add blossoms #'s 11 and 12. Glue red accent #'s 11a and 12a in place.
- Position Banner B leave and stem #'s 6-10 according to design, folding back the bottom of #6 to wrong side. Glue. Glue on light-green accent piece #'s 7a-10a. Position white blossom #'s 13, 14, 15 and glue. Add red accent #'s 13a, 14a, 15a and glue in place.
- Position letters using threads of burlap as a guide for straight lines. Glue.
- Place white arches #20 on each banner, folding back top to wrong side. Glue.
- Run thread of glue around each complete leaf using picture as guide, and press olive yarn on glue. On Banner B, the olive yarn runs all the way up the stem and around the bottom left leaf and back to bottom edge.
- Run another thread of glue along to top edge only of leaves and blossoms and press bright-yellow yarn along top edge.
- Run a thick line of glue along edge of each arch and press first a red, then a yellow piece of yarn close to the edge.
- Glue on white basic shape #'s 16 and 17 of butterfly.
- Glue on antennae #15.
- Place red dots #18 on wings and yellow dots #19 on smaller bottom wings. Glue.
- Outline entire butterfly with red yarn.
- Slip rod through rod pocket and hang.

Shining Star Publications, Copyright © 1992, A Division of Good Apple

SS2808

# GROW IN GRACE AND KNOWLEDGE
# OF OUR LORD AND SAVIOR JESUS CHRIST . . .

Banner A

Banner B

1″ = 1′

# GROW IN GRACE AND KNOWLEDGE
## OF OUR LORD AND SAVIOR JESUS CHRIST . . .

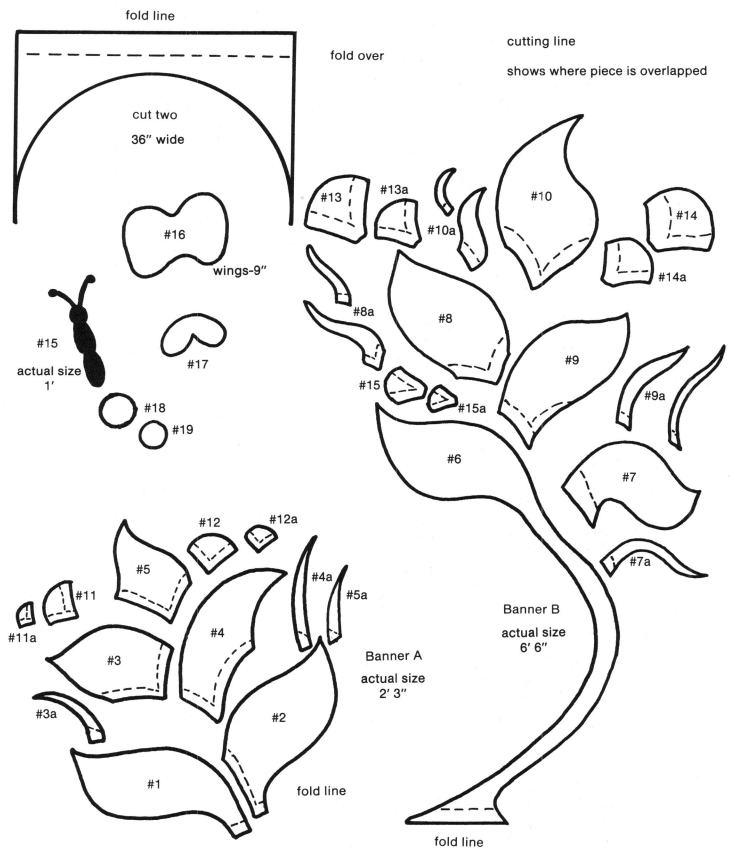

fold line

cut two
36" wide

fold over

cutting line

shows where piece is overlapped

#16

wings-9"

#15

actual size
1'

#17

#18

#19

#13

#13a

#10a

#10

#14

#14a

#8a

#8

#9

#9a

#15

#15a

#6

#7

#7a

#12

#12a

#5

#4a

#11

#5a

#11a

#4

#3

Banner A

actual size
2' 3"

Banner B

actual size
6' 6"

#3a

#2

#1

fold line

fold line

SS2808

# Grow in grace and knowledge of our Lord and Savior Jesus Christ

white letters

actual size
large letters-8″
small letters-6″

# To Him be glory both now and forever! Amen.

SS2808